50 Italian Restaurant Bread Recipes for Home

By: Kelly Johnson

Table of Contents

- Ciabatta
- Focaccia
- Pane Casereccio
- Pane Toscano
- Grissini
- Pane di Altamura
- Panettone
- Pandoro
- Piadina
- Pizza Bianca
- Pane di Matera
- Pugliese Bread
- Taralli
- Bruschetta
- Pane di Napoli
- Sfilatini
- Focaccia al Rosmarino
- Pane al Latte
- Pane di Semola
- Pane di Segale
- Panforte
- Gallette
- Rounds of Focaccia
- Focaccia alla Genovese
- Pane con Olio
- Pane Integrale
- Pizza Margherita Crust
- Pane di Cirié
- Pan Carré
- Focaccia al Pomodoro
- Pane di Orzo
- Pan di Zucchero

- Crescia
- Focaccia alla Barese
- Pane al Vino
- Pan di Spagna
- Pane di Patate
- Focaccia con Cipolle
- Focaccia al Rosmarino e Sale Grosso
- Pane di Biga
- Focaccia con Olive
- Pane alla Pugliese
- Pane al Lievito Madre
- Focaccia con Aglio
- Pane alla Griglia
- Pan di Mais
- Focaccia ai Formaggi
- Pane della Nonna
- Pane alla Romana
- Focaccia alle Erbe

Ciabatta

Ingredients:

For the Starter (Biga):

- 1/2 cup (65g) all-purpose flour
- 1/4 cup (60ml) water
- 1/4 tsp active dry yeast

For the Dough:

- 3 1/2 cups (450g) all-purpose flour
- 1 1/4 cups (300ml) water (room temperature)
- 1 tsp salt
- 1/4 tsp active dry yeast
- 1 tbsp olive oil
- Biga (from above)

Instructions:

1. **Prepare the Biga:**
    - Mix the flour, water, and yeast in a small bowl.
    - Cover with plastic wrap and let sit at room temperature for 12-16 hours or overnight. The biga should become bubbly and slightly risen.
2. **Make the Dough:**
    - In a large bowl, combine the flour, salt, and yeast.
    - Add the biga and water to the dry ingredients and mix until combined. The dough will be sticky and wet.
    - Knead the dough on a floured surface for about 10 minutes, or use a stand mixer with a dough hook for about 6-8 minutes. The dough should be elastic and smooth but still sticky.
3. **First Rise:**
    - Transfer the dough to a lightly oiled bowl, cover with plastic wrap, and let rise in a warm place for about 1 to 1.5 hours, or until doubled in size.
4. **Shape the Ciabatta:**
    - Gently deflate the dough and transfer it to a floured surface. Divide it into two equal parts.
    - Shape each part into a rough rectangle, being careful not to over-handle the dough to maintain its airy texture.
    - Transfer the shaped loaves to a parchment-lined baking sheet.
5. **Second Rise:**
    - Cover the loaves loosely with a clean towel and let them rise for about 30-45 minutes, or until slightly puffed.

6. **Preheat the Oven:**
    - Preheat your oven to 450°F (230°C). Place a pan of water on the bottom rack of the oven to create steam, which helps achieve a crisp crust.
7. **Bake:**
    - Brush the tops of the loaves with a little olive oil.
    - Bake for 20-25 minutes, or until the loaves are golden brown and sound hollow when tapped on the bottom.
    - Allow the ciabatta to cool on a wire rack before slicing.

Enjoy your homemade Ciabatta with olive oil, as a sandwich base, or however you prefer!

Focaccia

Ingredients:

For the Dough:

- 3 1/2 cups (450g) all-purpose flour
- 1 1/2 cups (360ml) warm water (110°F / 45°C)
- 1/4 cup (60ml) olive oil, plus extra for drizzling
- 2 tsp salt
- 2 tsp active dry yeast
- 1 tsp sugar

For Topping:

- 2 tbsp olive oil
- 1-2 tbsp coarse sea salt
- Fresh rosemary leaves or other herbs (optional)

Instructions:

1. **Prepare the Yeast Mixture:**
   - In a small bowl, dissolve the sugar in the warm water. Sprinkle the yeast on top and let it sit for about 5-10 minutes, or until it becomes frothy.
2. **Mix the Dough:**
   - In a large bowl, combine the flour and salt. Create a well in the center and pour in the yeast mixture and olive oil.
   - Mix until the dough starts to come together. If it's too sticky, add a little more flour; if too dry, add a bit more water.
3. **Knead the Dough:**
   - Transfer the dough to a floured surface and knead for about 8-10 minutes until it is smooth and elastic. Alternatively, use a stand mixer with a dough hook for about 5-7 minutes.
4. **First Rise:**
   - Place the dough in a lightly oiled bowl, cover with plastic wrap or a damp cloth, and let it rise in a warm place for about 1-1.5 hours, or until doubled in size.
5. **Prepare for Baking:**
   - Preheat your oven to 450°F (230°C).
   - Punch down the dough and transfer it to a well-oiled baking sheet or a baking pan. Stretch the dough to fit the pan, creating dimples with your fingers all over the surface.
6. **Add Toppings:**
   - Drizzle the top of the dough with olive oil, then sprinkle with coarse sea salt and rosemary leaves or other herbs if desired.

7. **Second Rise:**
   - Let the dough rise for another 20-30 minutes, or until slightly puffed.
8. **Bake:**
   - Bake in the preheated oven for 20-25 minutes, or until the focaccia is golden brown and sounds hollow when tapped on the bottom.
9. **Cool and Serve:**
   - Allow the focaccia to cool slightly on a wire rack before slicing and serving.

Enjoy your focaccia as a delicious appetizer, side dish, or base for sandwiches!

Pane Casereccio

Ingredients:

- **For the Starter:**
    - 1/2 cup (65g) all-purpose flour
    - 1/4 cup (60ml) water
    - 1/4 tsp active dry yeast
- **For the Dough:**
    - 3 1/2 cups (450g) all-purpose flour
    - 1 1/2 cups (360ml) warm water (110°F / 45°C)
    - 1 1/2 tsp salt
    - 1/2 tsp active dry yeast
    - 1 tbsp olive oil (optional, for a softer crumb)

Instructions:

1. **Prepare the Starter:**
    - In a small bowl, mix together the flour, water, and yeast.
    - Cover with plastic wrap or a damp cloth and let it sit at room temperature for 12-16 hours. The starter should become bubbly and slightly risen.
2. **Make the Dough:**
    - In a large mixing bowl, combine the flour and salt. Create a well in the center.
    - Add the starter and warm water to the well. If using, add the olive oil as well.
    - Mix until the dough begins to come together. It will be somewhat sticky.
3. **Knead the Dough:**
    - Transfer the dough to a floured surface and knead for about 10 minutes, or until the dough is smooth and elastic. Alternatively, use a stand mixer with a dough hook for about 6-8 minutes.
4. **First Rise:**
    - Place the dough in a lightly oiled bowl, cover with plastic wrap or a damp cloth, and let it rise in a warm place for about 1-1.5 hours, or until doubled in size.
5. **Shape the Bread:**
    - Punch down the dough and transfer it to a floured surface. Shape it into a round or oval loaf, depending on your preference.
    - Place the shaped dough onto a parchment-lined or lightly floured baking sheet.
6. **Second Rise:**
    - Cover the dough with a cloth and let it rise for another 30-45 minutes, or until slightly puffed.
7. **Preheat the Oven:**
    - Preheat your oven to 450°F (230°C).
8. **Bake the Bread:**

- Optional: Slash the top of the loaf with a sharp knife or razor blade to allow for expansion during baking.
- Bake the bread in the preheated oven for 25-35 minutes, or until the crust is golden brown and the loaf sounds hollow when tapped on the bottom.

9. **Cool and Serve:**
    - Allow the bread to cool on a wire rack before slicing.

Pane Casereccio is perfect for enjoying with a variety of toppings, dips, or as an accompaniment to soups and stews. Enjoy!

Pane Toscano

Ingredients:

- 3 1/2 cups (450g) all-purpose flour
- 1 1/2 cups (360ml) warm water (110°F / 45°C)
- 2 tsp active dry yeast
- 1 tsp sugar
- 1 tbsp olive oil (optional)
- 2 tsp salt (optional, for a salted version)

Instructions:

1. **Prepare the Yeast:**
    - In a small bowl, dissolve the sugar in the warm water. Sprinkle the yeast over the top and let it sit for about 5-10 minutes until frothy.
2. **Mix the Dough:**
    - In a large bowl, combine the flour and salt if using.
    - Create a well in the center and pour in the yeast mixture and olive oil (if using).
    - Mix until a shaggy dough forms. Add more flour if needed to bring the dough together.
3. **Knead the Dough:**
    - Transfer the dough to a floured surface and knead for about 10 minutes, or until smooth and elastic. Alternatively, use a stand mixer with a dough hook for 6-8 minutes.
4. **First Rise:**
    - Place the dough in a lightly oiled bowl, cover with plastic wrap or a damp cloth, and let it rise in a warm place for about 1-1.5 hours, or until doubled in size.
5. **Shape the Bread:**
    - Punch down the dough and transfer it to a floured surface. Shape it into a round or oval loaf.
    - Place the shaped dough onto a parchment-lined or lightly floured baking sheet.
6. **Second Rise:**
    - Cover the dough with a cloth and let it rise for another 30-45 minutes, or until slightly puffed.
7. **Preheat the Oven:**
    - Preheat your oven to 450°F (230°C).
8. **Bake the Bread:**
    - Slash the top of the loaf with a sharp knife or razor blade to allow for expansion.
    - Bake for 25-35 minutes, or until the crust is golden brown and the loaf sounds hollow when tapped on the bottom.
9. **Cool and Serve:**
    - Allow the bread to cool on a wire rack before slicing.

Pane Toscano is great with cheeses, meats, or just a drizzle of olive oil. Enjoy!

Grissini

Ingredients:

- 2 1/4 tsp active dry yeast
- 1 1/2 cups (360ml) warm water (110°F / 45°C)
- 3 1/2 cups (450g) all-purpose flour
- 2 tbsp olive oil
- 1 tsp salt
- 1 tbsp sugar
- Coarse sea salt (for sprinkling)

Instructions:

1. **Prepare the Yeast:**
   - In a small bowl, dissolve the sugar in warm water. Sprinkle the yeast over the top and let it sit for about 5-10 minutes until frothy.
2. **Mix the Dough:**
   - In a large bowl, combine the flour and salt.
   - Create a well in the center and pour in the yeast mixture and olive oil.
   - Mix until a dough forms.
3. **Knead the Dough:**
   - Turn the dough out onto a floured surface and knead for about 7-10 minutes, or until smooth and elastic. Alternatively, use a stand mixer with a dough hook for about 5-7 minutes.
4. **First Rise:**
   - Place the dough in a lightly oiled bowl, cover with plastic wrap or a damp cloth, and let it rise in a warm place for about 1-1.5 hours, or until doubled in size.
5. **Shape the Grissini:**
   - Punch down the dough and transfer it to a floured surface. Roll it out into a rectangle about 1/4 inch thick.
   - Cut the dough into thin strips, about 1/2 inch wide.
   - Gently stretch each strip to the desired length and place them on a parchment-lined baking sheet.
6. **Second Rise:**
   - Let the grissini rise for about 20 minutes.
7. **Preheat the Oven:**
   - Preheat your oven to 400°F (200°C).
8. **Bake:**
   - Brush the grissini with a little olive oil and sprinkle with coarse sea salt.
   - Bake for 12-15 minutes, or until golden and crisp.
9. **Cool and Serve:**
   - Let the grissini cool on a wire rack before serving.

Grissini are perfect as an appetizer, snack, or accompaniment to soups and salads. Enjoy!

Pane di Altamura

Ingredients:

- **For the Starter (Lievito Madre):**
    - 1/2 cup (65g) durum wheat flour
    - 1/4 cup (60ml) warm water
    - 1/4 tsp active dry yeast
- **For the Dough:**
    - 3 1/2 cups (450g) durum wheat flour
    - 1 1/2 cups (360ml) warm water
    - 1 1/2 tsp salt
    - 1/4 tsp active dry yeast
    - 1 tbsp olive oil (optional)

Instructions:

1. **Prepare the Starter:**
    - In a small bowl, mix the durum wheat flour, water, and yeast. Cover with plastic wrap and let it sit at room temperature for 12-16 hours or overnight.
2. **Make the Dough:**
    - In a large bowl, combine the durum wheat flour and salt. Create a well in the center.
    - Add the starter, warm water, and olive oil (if using) to the well.
    - Mix until the dough starts to come together.
3. **Knead the Dough:**
    - Turn the dough out onto a floured surface and knead for about 10 minutes, or until smooth and elastic. Alternatively, use a stand mixer with a dough hook for about 6-8 minutes.
4. **First Rise:**
    - Place the dough in a lightly oiled bowl, cover with plastic wrap or a damp cloth, and let it rise in a warm place for 1-1.5 hours, or until doubled in size.
5. **Shape the Bread:**
    - Punch down the dough and shape it into a round loaf.
    - Place the shaped dough onto a parchment-lined or lightly floured baking sheet.
6. **Second Rise:**
    - Cover the dough with a cloth and let it rise for another 30-45 minutes.
7. **Preheat the Oven:**
    - Preheat your oven to 450°F (230°C).
8. **Bake the Bread:**
    - Optional: Slash the top of the loaf with a sharp knife for a classic look.
    - Bake for 30-35 minutes, or until the crust is golden brown and the loaf sounds hollow when tapped on the bottom.

9. **Cool and Serve:**
    - Let the bread cool on a wire rack before slicing.

Pane di Altamura has a distinct flavor and crust, perfect for enjoying with cheeses, cured meats, or simply with olive oil. Enjoy!

Panettone

Ingredients:

For the Starter:

- 1/4 cup (30g) all-purpose flour
- 1/4 cup (60ml) warm water
- 1/4 tsp active dry yeast

For the Dough:

- 3 1/2 cups (450g) all-purpose flour
- 1/2 cup (100g) sugar
- 1/2 cup (115g) unsalted butter, softened
- 1 cup (240ml) warm milk
- 4 large eggs
- 1 tsp vanilla extract
- 1 tsp grated lemon zest
- 1/2 tsp grated orange zest
- 1/4 tsp salt
- 1/2 cup (75g) mixed dried fruits or raisins
- 1/2 cup (75g) candied orange peel, chopped
- 1/2 cup (75g) chopped nuts (optional)

For the Glaze:

- 1/4 cup (30g) all-purpose flour
- 2 tbsp sugar
- 1/4 cup (60ml) water

Instructions:

1. **Prepare the Starter:**
     - In a small bowl, mix the flour, warm water, and yeast. Cover with plastic wrap and let it sit at room temperature for 1-2 hours, or until bubbly and active.
2. **Make the Dough:**
     - In a large bowl, combine the flour, sugar, and salt. Create a well in the center.
     - Add the starter, warm milk, eggs, butter, vanilla, lemon zest, and orange zest to the well.
     - Mix until the dough begins to come together. Add the dried fruits, candied orange peel, and nuts, and knead until fully incorporated. The dough will be sticky.
3. **Knead and First Rise:**
     - Turn the dough onto a floured surface and knead for about 10 minutes, or until smooth and elastic. Alternatively, use a stand mixer with a dough hook for about 6-8 minutes.
     - Place the dough in a lightly oiled bowl, cover with plastic wrap or a damp cloth, and let it rise in a warm place for 2-3 hours, or until doubled in size.

4. **Shape and Second Rise:**
    - Punch down the dough and transfer it to a lightly floured surface. Shape it into a round loaf.
    - Place the dough into a panettone mold or a lined tall baking pan. Cover with a cloth and let it rise for another 1-2 hours.
5. **Preheat the Oven:**
    - Preheat your oven to 350°F (175°C).
6. **Prepare the Glaze:**
    - In a small bowl, mix the flour, sugar, and water to form a smooth paste. Spread the glaze over the top of the risen dough.
7. **Bake:**
    - Bake the panettone in the preheated oven for 45-60 minutes, or until golden brown and a toothpick inserted into the center comes out clean.
8. **Cool and Serve:**
    - Allow the panettone to cool completely on a wire rack before slicing.

Panettone is perfect for holiday celebrations, enjoyed with coffee or as part of festive meals. Enjoy!

Pandoro

Ingredients:

For the Starter:

- 1/2 cup (65g) all-purpose flour
- 1/4 cup (60ml) warm water
- 1/4 tsp active dry yeast

For the Dough:

- 3 1/2 cups (450g) all-purpose flour
- 1 cup (200g) sugar
- 1 cup (230g) unsalted butter, softened
- 1 cup (240ml) warm milk
- 4 large eggs
- 1 tsp vanilla extract
- 1 tsp grated lemon zest
- 1/2 tsp salt

For the Glaze:

- 1/4 cup (30g) all-purpose flour
- 2 tbsp sugar
- 1/4 cup (60ml) water

Instructions:

1. **Prepare the Starter:**
   - In a small bowl, mix the flour, warm water, and yeast. Cover and let sit at room temperature for 1-2 hours, or until bubbly.
2. **Make the Dough:**
   - In a large bowl, combine the flour and sugar. Make a well in the center.
   - Add the starter, warm milk, eggs, butter, vanilla extract, lemon zest, and salt to the well.
   - Mix until a sticky dough forms. Knead the dough for about 10 minutes on a floured surface or use a stand mixer with a dough hook for 6-8 minutes until smooth and elastic.
3. **First Rise:**
   - Place the dough in a lightly oiled bowl, cover with plastic wrap or a damp cloth, and let it rise in a warm place for 2-3 hours, or until doubled in size.
4. **Shape and Second Rise:**

- Punch down the dough and transfer it to a floured surface. Shape it into a ball and place it in a greased and floured Pandoro mold or a well-greased tall cake pan.
- Cover with a cloth and let it rise for another 1-2 hours.

5. **Preheat the Oven:**
   - Preheat your oven to 350°F (175°C).
6. **Prepare the Glaze:**
   - In a small bowl, mix the flour, sugar, and water to create a smooth paste. Spread the glaze over the top of the risen dough.
7. **Bake:**
   - Bake in the preheated oven for 45-60 minutes, or until the Pandoro is golden brown and a toothpick inserted into the center comes out clean.
8. **Cool and Serve:**
   - Allow the Pandoro to cool in the mold for 15 minutes, then transfer to a wire rack to cool completely. Dust with powdered sugar before serving.

Pandoro is perfect for festive occasions, served with a dusting of powdered sugar or alongside a glass of sparkling wine. Enjoy!

Piadina

Ingredients:

- 2 1/2 cups (320g) all-purpose flour
- 1/2 cup (120ml) water
- 1/4 cup (60ml) lard or unsalted butter (softened)
- 1 tsp salt
- 1/2 tsp baking powder (optional, for a softer texture)

Instructions:

1. **Prepare the Dough:**
   - In a large bowl, combine the flour, salt, and baking powder (if using).
   - Add the lard or butter and mix until the mixture resembles coarse crumbs.
   - Gradually add the water, mixing until a soft dough forms. You may need a little more or less water depending on the flour and humidity.
2. **Knead the Dough:**
   - Turn the dough out onto a floured surface and knead for about 5 minutes, or until smooth and elastic.
   - Cover the dough with a damp cloth and let it rest for at least 30 minutes at room temperature.
3. **Shape the Piadine:**
   - Divide the dough into 4 equal pieces.
   - Roll each piece out into a thin circle, about 1/8 inch (3mm) thick. Aim for a diameter of about 8-10 inches (20-25 cm).
4. **Cook the Piadine:**
   - Heat a large, dry skillet or griddle over medium-high heat.
   - Cook each piadina for 1-2 minutes on each side, or until golden brown spots appear and the bread is cooked through. Adjust the heat if necessary to prevent burning.
5. **Serve:**
   - Keep the piadine warm in a cloth while you cook the others.
   - Serve immediately with your choice of fillings, such as prosciutto, cheese, arugula, or roasted vegetables.

Piadina is great for sandwiches or as an accompaniment to salads and soups. Enjoy!

Pizza Bianca

Ingredients:

For the Dough:

- 2 1/4 tsp active dry yeast
- 1 1/2 cups (360ml) warm water (110°F / 45°C)
- 3 1/2 cups (450g) all-purpose flour
- 2 tbsp olive oil
- 1 tsp salt
- 1 tsp sugar

For the Topping:

- 2-3 tbsp olive oil
- 1-2 cloves garlic, minced
- 1 tsp fresh rosemary leaves (or dried if fresh isn't available)
- 1/2 cup (50g) grated Parmesan or Pecorino cheese
- Coarse sea salt (for sprinkling)

Instructions:

1. **Prepare the Dough:**
    - In a small bowl, dissolve the sugar in the warm water. Sprinkle the yeast over the top and let it sit for about 5-10 minutes, or until frothy.
    - In a large bowl, combine the flour and salt. Create a well in the center and add the yeast mixture and olive oil.
    - Mix until a dough forms, then turn it out onto a floured surface and knead for about 8-10 minutes, or until smooth and elastic. Alternatively, use a stand mixer with a dough hook for about 5-7 minutes.
2. **First Rise:**
    - Place the dough in a lightly oiled bowl, cover with plastic wrap or a damp cloth, and let it rise in a warm place for 1-1.5 hours, or until doubled in size.
3. **Preheat the Oven:**
    - Preheat your oven to 475°F (245°C). If you have a pizza stone, place it in the oven to preheat as well.
4. **Shape the Dough:**
    - Punch down the dough and transfer it to a floured surface. Roll it out into a rectangle or circle about 1/4 inch (6mm) thick.
    - Transfer the rolled dough to a parchment-lined baking sheet or a preheated pizza stone.
5. **Add the Toppings:**
    - Brush the surface of the dough with olive oil.

- - Sprinkle the minced garlic, rosemary, and grated cheese evenly over the top.
  - Season with coarse sea salt to taste.
6. **Bake:**
   - Bake in the preheated oven for 12-15 minutes, or until the crust is golden and crisp and the cheese is melted.
7. **Cool and Serve:**
   - Let the Pizza Bianca cool slightly on a wire rack before slicing.

This simple yet flavorful flatbread is perfect as an appetizer, side dish, or even a light meal. Enjoy!

Pane di Matera

Ingredients:

For the Starter (Lievito Madre):

- 1/2 cup (65g) all-purpose flour
- 1/4 cup (60ml) water
- 1/4 tsp active dry yeast

For the Dough:

- 3 1/2 cups (450g) all-purpose flour
- 1 1/2 cups (360ml) warm water (110°F / 45°C)
- 1 1/2 tsp salt
- 1/4 tsp active dry yeast
- 1 tbsp olive oil (optional, for a softer crumb)

Instructions:

1. **Prepare the Starter:**
   - In a small bowl, combine the flour, water, and yeast. Stir until smooth, cover with plastic wrap or a damp cloth, and let it sit at room temperature for 12-16 hours, or until bubbly and slightly risen.
2. **Make the Dough:**
   - In a large bowl, combine the flour and salt. Create a well in the center.
   - Add the starter, warm water, and olive oil (if using) to the well.
   - Mix until a sticky dough forms. You may need to adjust the amount of flour or water depending on your dough's consistency.
3. **Knead the Dough:**
   - Turn the dough onto a floured surface and knead for about 10 minutes, or until smooth and elastic. Alternatively, use a stand mixer with a dough hook for about 6-8 minutes.
4. **First Rise:**
   - Place the dough in a lightly oiled bowl, cover with plastic wrap or a damp cloth, and let it rise in a warm place for about 1.5-2 hours, or until doubled in size.
5. **Shape the Bread:**
   - Punch down the dough and transfer it to a floured surface. Shape it into a round or oval loaf.
   - Place the shaped dough onto a parchment-lined or floured baking sheet.
6. **Second Rise:**
   - Cover the dough with a cloth and let it rise for another 45 minutes to 1 hour.
7. **Preheat the Oven:**
   - Preheat your oven to 450°F (230°C).

8. **Bake the Bread:**
    - Optional: Slash the top of the loaf with a sharp knife or razor blade to allow for expansion.
    - Bake for 25-35 minutes, or until the crust is golden brown and the bread sounds hollow when tapped on the bottom.
9. **Cool and Serve:**
    - Let the bread cool on a wire rack before slicing.

Pane di Matera is perfect with a variety of Italian dishes, or simply enjoyed with olive oil and cheese. Buon appetito!

Pugliese Bread

Ingredients:

For the Starter (Biga):

- 1/2 cup (65g) all-purpose flour
- 1/4 cup (60ml) water
- 1/4 tsp active dry yeast

For the Dough:

- 3 1/2 cups (450g) all-purpose flour
- 1 1/2 cups (360ml) warm water (110°F / 45°C)
- 2 tsp salt
- 1/2 tsp active dry yeast
- 1 tbsp olive oil

Instructions:

1. **Prepare the Starter:**
   - In a small bowl, combine the flour, water, and yeast. Mix until smooth.
   - Cover with plastic wrap and let it sit at room temperature for 12-16 hours, or until bubbly and doubled in size.
2. **Make the Dough:**
   - In a large bowl, mix the flour and salt.
   - Add the starter, warm water, yeast, and olive oil. Mix until a sticky dough forms.
   - Turn the dough onto a floured surface and knead for about 8-10 minutes, or until smooth and elastic. Alternatively, use a stand mixer with a dough hook for 6-8 minutes.
3. **First Rise:**
   - Place the dough in a lightly oiled bowl, cover with plastic wrap or a damp cloth, and let it rise in a warm place for 1.5-2 hours, or until doubled in size.
4. **Shape the Bread:**
   - Punch down the dough and transfer it to a floured surface. Shape it into a round or oval loaf.
   - Place the dough on a parchment-lined or floured baking sheet.
5. **Second Rise:**
   - Cover the dough with a cloth and let it rise for another 45 minutes to 1 hour.
6. **Preheat the Oven:**
   - Preheat your oven to 450°F (230°C).
7. **Bake the Bread:**
   - Optional: Slash the top of the loaf with a sharp knife or razor blade for a traditional look.

- Bake for 25-35 minutes, or until the crust is golden brown and the loaf sounds hollow when tapped on the bottom.
8. **Cool and Serve:**
    - Allow the bread to cool on a wire rack before slicing.

Pugliese Bread is fantastic for sandwiches, or simply enjoyed with olive oil and your favorite accompaniments. Enjoy!

Taralli

Ingredients:

- 3 cups (375g) all-purpose flour
- 1/2 cup (120ml) dry white wine
- 1/2 cup (120ml) olive oil
- 1 tsp salt
- 1/2 tsp black pepper (optional)
- 1/2 tsp fennel seeds or caraway seeds (optional, for traditional flavor)
- 1 large egg (for egg wash, optional)

Instructions:

1. **Prepare the Dough:**
    - In a large bowl, combine the flour, salt, pepper, and fennel or caraway seeds if using.
    - Make a well in the center and add the wine and olive oil.
    - Mix until the dough comes together. You may need to adjust the flour or liquid slightly to achieve a firm, slightly sticky dough.
2. **Knead the Dough:**
    - Turn the dough onto a floured surface and knead for about 5 minutes, or until smooth and elastic.
    - Cover the dough with a cloth and let it rest for 30 minutes.
3. **Shape the Taralli:**
    - Preheat your oven to 375°F (190°C).
    - Divide the dough into small pieces (about 1 tablespoon each). Roll each piece into a small rope, then form into a ring, pinching the ends together.
    - Place the shaped taralli onto a parchment-lined baking sheet.
4. **Optional Egg Wash:**
    - For a shinier finish, brush the taralli with a beaten egg before baking.
5. **Bake:**
    - Bake for 20-25 minutes, or until golden brown and crisp.
6. **Cool and Serve:**
    - Allow the taralli to cool completely on a wire rack before serving.

Taralli are great for snacking on their own or as a crunchy addition to a cheese platter. Enjoy!

Bruschetta

Ingredients:

- 1 loaf of Italian bread (such as ciabatta or baguette)
- 4-5 ripe tomatoes, finely chopped
- 2-3 cloves garlic, minced
- 1/4 cup (60ml) extra-virgin olive oil
- 1/4 cup fresh basil leaves, chopped
- Salt and pepper, to taste
- Balsamic vinegar (optional, for drizzling)

Instructions:

1. **Prepare the Bread:**
    - Preheat your oven to 400°F (200°C).
    - Slice the loaf of bread into 1/2-inch thick slices.
    - Place the slices on a baking sheet and toast in the oven for about 5-7 minutes, or until golden and crisp.
2. **Prepare the Topping:**
    - In a bowl, combine the chopped tomatoes, minced garlic, olive oil, and chopped basil.
    - Season with salt and pepper to taste. Mix well.
3. **Assemble the Bruschetta:**
    - Spoon the tomato mixture onto the toasted bread slices.
4. **Optional:**
    - Drizzle with a small amount of balsamic vinegar if desired.
5. **Serve:**
    - Serve immediately while the bread is still warm and crispy.

Bruschetta is perfect as an appetizer or a light snack, showcasing the fresh flavors of summer. Enjoy!

Pane di Napoli

Ingredients:

- 3 1/2 cups (450g) all-purpose flour
- 1 1/2 cups (360ml) warm water (110°F / 45°C)
- 2 tsp salt
- 1/4 tsp active dry yeast
- 1 tbsp olive oil (optional)

Instructions:

1. **Prepare the Dough:**
    - In a small bowl, dissolve the yeast in warm water and let it sit for 5-10 minutes until frothy.
    - In a large bowl, combine the flour and salt.
    - Make a well in the center and add the yeast mixture and olive oil (if using).
    - Mix until a sticky dough forms. You may need to adjust the amount of flour or water to get the right consistency.
2. **Knead the Dough:**
    - Turn the dough onto a floured surface and knead for about 10 minutes until smooth and elastic. Alternatively, use a stand mixer with a dough hook for about 6-8 minutes.
3. **First Rise:**
    - Place the dough in a lightly oiled bowl, cover with plastic wrap or a damp cloth, and let it rise in a warm place for 1.5-2 hours, or until doubled in size.
4. **Shape the Bread:**
    - Punch down the dough and transfer it to a floured surface. Shape it into a round or oval loaf.
    - Place the shaped dough on a parchment-lined or floured baking sheet.
5. **Second Rise:**
    - Cover the dough with a cloth and let it rise for another 45 minutes to 1 hour.
6. **Preheat the Oven:**
    - Preheat your oven to 450°F (230°C).
7. **Bake the Bread:**
    - Optional: Slash the top of the loaf with a sharp knife to allow for expansion.
    - Bake for 30-35 minutes, or until the crust is golden brown and the bread sounds hollow when tapped on the bottom.
8. **Cool and Serve:**
    - Let the bread cool on a wire rack before slicing.

Pane di Napoli is perfect for enjoying with cheese, cured meats, or as a side to any meal. Enjoy!

Sfilatini

Ingredients:

- 2 1/2 cups (320g) all-purpose flour
- 1 cup (240ml) warm water (110°F / 45°C)
- 1/4 cup (60ml) olive oil
- 1 tsp sugar
- 1 tsp salt
- 1/4 tsp active dry yeast
- Coarse sea salt (for sprinkling)

Instructions:

1. **Prepare the Dough:**
    - In a small bowl, dissolve the sugar in the warm water. Sprinkle the yeast over the top and let it sit for about 5-10 minutes, until frothy.
    - In a large bowl, combine the flour and salt.
    - Make a well in the center and add the yeast mixture and olive oil.
    - Mix until a dough forms. It will be slightly sticky.
2. **Knead the Dough:**
    - Turn the dough onto a floured surface and knead for about 5-7 minutes, until smooth and elastic. Alternatively, use a stand mixer with a dough hook for about 4-5 minutes.
3. **First Rise:**
    - Place the dough in a lightly oiled bowl, cover with plastic wrap or a damp cloth, and let it rise in a warm place for 1-1.5 hours, or until doubled in size.
4. **Shape the Sfilatini:**
    - Preheat your oven to 375°F (190°C).
    - Punch down the dough and transfer it to a floured surface.
    - Roll out the dough into a rectangle about 1/4 inch (6mm) thick.
    - Using a sharp knife or a pizza cutter, cut the dough into thin strips, about 1/2 inch (1.5 cm) wide.
5. **Prepare for Baking:**
    - Place the strips onto a parchment-lined baking sheet.
    - Lightly brush with olive oil and sprinkle with coarse sea salt.
6. **Bake the Sfilatini:**
    - Bake for 15-20 minutes, or until the breadsticks are golden brown and crispy.
7. **Cool and Serve:**
    - Let the Sfilatini cool on a wire rack before serving.

These crispy breadsticks are perfect for dipping in olive oil, serving with cheese, or just enjoying on their own. Buon appetito!

Focaccia al Rosmarino

Ingredients:

For the Dough:

- 3 1/2 cups (450g) all-purpose flour
- 1 1/2 cups (360ml) warm water (110°F / 45°C)
- 1/4 cup (60ml) extra-virgin olive oil (plus extra for drizzling)
- 2 tsp salt
- 1 tsp sugar
- 1/4 tsp active dry yeast

For Topping:

- 2-3 tbsp fresh rosemary leaves (or dried if fresh isn't available)
- Coarse sea salt (for sprinkling)
- Extra olive oil (for drizzling)

Instructions:

1. **Prepare the Dough:**
    - In a small bowl, dissolve the sugar in the warm water. Sprinkle the yeast over the top and let it sit for about 5-10 minutes, or until frothy.
    - In a large bowl, combine the flour and salt.
    - Make a well in the center and add the yeast mixture and olive oil.
    - Mix until a sticky dough forms. Adjust the amount of flour or water as needed.
2. **Knead the Dough:**
    - Turn the dough onto a floured surface and knead for about 8-10 minutes, until smooth and elastic. Alternatively, use a stand mixer with a dough hook for 6-8 minutes.
3. **First Rise:**
    - Place the dough in a lightly oiled bowl, cover with plastic wrap or a damp cloth, and let it rise in a warm place for 1-1.5 hours, or until doubled in size.
4. **Shape the Focaccia:**
    - Preheat your oven to 450°F (230°C).
    - Punch down the dough and transfer it to a parchment-lined baking sheet.
    - Gently stretch and press the dough out to fit the baking sheet, about 1/2 inch (1.5 cm) thick.
5. **Add Toppings:**
    - Dimple the surface of the dough with your fingers.
    - Drizzle generously with olive oil.
    - Scatter the rosemary leaves and sprinkle with coarse sea salt.
6. **Second Rise:**

- Let the dough rise for another 20-30 minutes, covered with a cloth.
7. **Bake:**
    - Bake in the preheated oven for 20-25 minutes, or until the focaccia is golden brown and the edges are crisp.
8. **Cool and Serve:**
    - Allow the focaccia to cool slightly on a wire rack before slicing.

Focaccia al Rosmarino is perfect as an appetizer, side dish, or just enjoyed with a bit of extra olive oil. Enjoy!

Pane al Latte

Ingredients:

- 4 cups (500g) all-purpose flour
- 1 cup (240ml) whole milk, warmed
- 1/4 cup (60ml) unsalted butter, softened
- 1/4 cup (50g) sugar
- 2 tsp active dry yeast
- 1 tsp salt
- 1 large egg

Instructions:

1. **Prepare the Yeast Mixture:**
   - In a small bowl, dissolve 1 tablespoon of sugar in the warm milk. Sprinkle the yeast over the top and let it sit for about 5-10 minutes, or until frothy.
2. **Prepare the Dough:**
   - In a large bowl, combine the flour, remaining sugar, and salt.
   - Make a well in the center and add the yeast mixture, softened butter, and the egg.
   - Mix until the dough comes together, then turn it out onto a floured surface and knead for about 8-10 minutes, or until smooth and elastic. Alternatively, use a stand mixer with a dough hook for 6-8 minutes.
3. **First Rise:**
   - Place the dough in a lightly oiled bowl, cover with plastic wrap or a damp cloth, and let it rise in a warm place for 1-1.5 hours, or until doubled in size.
4. **Shape the Bread:**
   - Punch down the dough and turn it out onto a floured surface.
   - Shape the dough into a loaf by rolling it into a rectangle, then folding the sides over and rolling it up from the bottom. Pinch the seams to seal.
   - Place the shaped dough into a greased 9x5-inch (23x13 cm) loaf pan.
5. **Second Rise:**
   - Cover the loaf pan with a cloth and let the dough rise for another 30-45 minutes, or until it has risen above the edge of the pan.
6. **Preheat the Oven:**
   - Preheat your oven to 350°F (175°C).
7. **Bake:**
   - Bake the bread for 30-35 minutes, or until golden brown and the loaf sounds hollow when tapped on the bottom.
8. **Cool and Serve:**
   - Allow the bread to cool in the pan for about 10 minutes, then transfer it to a wire rack to cool completely before slicing.

Pane al Latte is perfect for making sandwiches, or just enjoying with a bit of butter or jam. Buon appetito!

Pane di Semola

Ingredients:

- 2 1/2 cups (320g) semolina flour
- 1 1/2 cups (360ml) warm water (110°F / 45°C)
- 1/4 cup (60ml) olive oil
- 2 tsp salt
- 1 tsp sugar
- 1/4 tsp active dry yeast

Instructions:

1. **Prepare the Yeast Mixture:**
    - In a small bowl, dissolve the sugar in the warm water. Sprinkle the yeast over the top and let it sit for about 5-10 minutes, or until frothy.
2. **Prepare the Dough:**
    - In a large bowl, combine the semolina flour and salt.
    - Make a well in the center and add the yeast mixture and olive oil.
    - Mix until a sticky dough forms. You may need to adjust the amount of water or flour to get the right consistency.
3. **Knead the Dough:**
    - Turn the dough onto a floured surface and knead for about 8-10 minutes, or until smooth and elastic. Alternatively, use a stand mixer with a dough hook for 6-8 minutes.
4. **First Rise:**
    - Place the dough in a lightly oiled bowl, cover with plastic wrap or a damp cloth, and let it rise in a warm place for 1.5-2 hours, or until doubled in size.
5. **Shape the Bread:**
    - Punch down the dough and transfer it to a floured surface.
    - Shape the dough into a round or oval loaf.
    - Place the shaped dough onto a parchment-lined or floured baking sheet.
6. **Second Rise:**
    - Cover the dough with a cloth and let it rise for another 45 minutes to 1 hour.
7. **Preheat the Oven:**
    - Preheat your oven to 450°F (230°C).
8. **Bake:**
    - Optional: Slash the top of the loaf with a sharp knife to allow for expansion.
    - Bake for 25-35 minutes, or until the crust is golden brown and the bread sounds hollow when tapped on the bottom.
9. **Cool and Serve:**
    - Allow the bread to cool on a wire rack before slicing.

Pane di Semola is great for enjoying with soups, stews, or just with a drizzle of olive oil. Enjoy!

Pane di Segale

Ingredients:

- 2 cups (250g) rye flour
- 1 1/2 cups (360ml) warm water (110°F / 45°C)
- 1 1/2 cups (200g) all-purpose flour
- 1 tbsp olive oil
- 1 tsp salt
- 1 tsp sugar
- 2 tsp active dry yeast

Instructions:

1. **Prepare the Yeast Mixture:**
    - In a small bowl, dissolve the sugar in the warm water. Sprinkle the yeast over the top and let it sit for about 5-10 minutes, or until frothy.
2. **Prepare the Dough:**
    - In a large bowl, combine the rye flour, all-purpose flour, and salt.
    - Make a well in the center and add the yeast mixture and olive oil.
    - Mix until a sticky dough forms. You may need to adjust the amount of water or flour to get the right consistency.
3. **Knead the Dough:**
    - Turn the dough onto a floured surface and knead for about 8-10 minutes, or until smooth and elastic. Alternatively, use a stand mixer with a dough hook for 6-8 minutes.
4. **First Rise:**
    - Place the dough in a lightly oiled bowl, cover with plastic wrap or a damp cloth, and let it rise in a warm place for 1.5-2 hours, or until doubled in size.
5. **Shape the Bread:**
    - Punch down the dough and transfer it to a floured surface.
    - Shape the dough into a round or oval loaf.
    - Place the shaped dough onto a parchment-lined or floured baking sheet.
6. **Second Rise:**
    - Cover the dough with a cloth and let it rise for another 45 minutes to 1 hour.
7. **Preheat the Oven:**
    - Preheat your oven to 425°F (220°C).
8. **Bake:**
    - Optional: Slash the top of the loaf with a sharp knife to allow for expansion.
    - Bake for 30-35 minutes, or until the crust is dark brown and the bread sounds hollow when tapped on the bottom.
9. **Cool and Serve:**
    - Allow the bread to cool on a wire rack before slicing.

Pane di Segale is perfect for sandwiches, served with cheese, or enjoyed with hearty soups. Buon appetito!

Panforte

Ingredients:

- **Nuts and Fruit:**
  - 1 cup (100g) almonds, whole or chopped
  - 1 cup (100g) walnuts, chopped
  - 1/2 cup (70g) candied orange peel, chopped
  - 1/2 cup (70g) candied lemon peel, chopped
  - 1/2 cup (70g) dried figs, chopped
  - 1/2 cup (70g) dried apricots, chopped
- **Dry Ingredients:**
  - 1 cup (130g) all-purpose flour
  - 1/2 cup (60g) cocoa powder
  - 1 tsp ground cinnamon
  - 1/2 tsp ground cloves
  - 1/4 tsp ground nutmeg
  - 1/4 tsp salt
- **Wet Ingredients:**
  - 1 cup (200g) sugar
  - 1/2 cup (120ml) honey
  - 1/4 cup (60ml) water
- **Additional:**
  - Powdered sugar (for dusting)

Instructions:

1. **Prepare the Ingredients:**
   - Preheat your oven to 325°F (160°C).
   - Line an 8-inch (20 cm) round cake pan with parchment paper and lightly grease it.
2. **Mix Nuts and Fruit:**
   - In a large bowl, combine the almonds, walnuts, candied orange peel, candied lemon peel, dried figs, and dried apricots.
3. **Combine Dry Ingredients:**
   - In another bowl, whisk together the flour, cocoa powder, cinnamon, cloves, nutmeg, and salt.
4. **Prepare the Syrup:**
   - In a small saucepan, combine the sugar, honey, and water.
   - Heat over medium heat, stirring occasionally, until the mixture comes to a boil.
   - Continue to cook for about 5 minutes, or until the syrup reaches 240°F (115°C) on a candy thermometer.
5. **Combine All Ingredients:**
   - Pour the hot syrup over the nut and fruit mixture.
   - Stir well to combine.
   - Add the dry ingredients and mix until fully incorporated. The batter will be thick.
6. **Bake the Panforte:**

- Pour the mixture into the prepared cake pan and spread it evenly.
- Bake for 35-40 minutes, or until the center is set and the edges are firm.

7. **Cool and Serve:**
    - Allow the panforte to cool in the pan for about 10 minutes.
    - Transfer to a wire rack and let it cool completely.
    - Dust with powdered sugar before serving.

Panforte keeps well for several weeks and often tastes even better after a few days as the flavors meld together. It can be served in small slices or chunks and makes a wonderful gift or festive treat. Enjoy!

Gallette

Ingredients:

For the Dough:

- 1 1/2 cups (190g) all-purpose flour
- 1/4 cup (50g) granulated sugar
- 1/2 tsp salt
- 1/2 cup (115g) unsalted butter, chilled and cut into small pieces
- 1/4 cup (60ml) ice water (more if needed)

For the Filling:

- 2 cups fresh fruit (e.g., berries, sliced apples, or peaches)
- 1/4 cup (50g) granulated sugar (adjust based on fruit sweetness)
- 1 tbsp all-purpose flour or cornstarch
- 1 tsp lemon juice (optional)
- 1/2 tsp ground cinnamon (optional)

For Topping:

- 1 egg, beaten (for egg wash)
- 1 tbsp coarse sugar (for sprinkling)

Instructions:

1. **Prepare the Dough:**
    - In a large bowl, whisk together the flour, sugar, and salt.
    - Cut in the butter using a pastry cutter or your fingers until the mixture resembles coarse crumbs.
    - Gradually add the ice water, mixing just until the dough comes together. Avoid overmixing.
    - Shape the dough into a disk, wrap in plastic wrap, and refrigerate for at least 30 minutes.
2. **Prepare the Filling:**
    - In a bowl, combine the fruit, sugar, flour or cornstarch, lemon juice, and cinnamon (if using). Mix well and set aside.
3. **Preheat the Oven:**
    - Preheat your oven to 375°F (190°C).
4. **Roll Out the Dough:**
    - On a lightly floured surface, roll out the dough into a 12-inch (30 cm) circle.
    - Transfer the dough to a parchment-lined baking sheet.
5. **Assemble the Galette:**

     - Spoon the fruit mixture into the center of the dough, leaving a 2-inch (5 cm) border around the edges.
     - Fold the edges of the dough over the fruit, pleating as you go to form a rustic tart shape.
6. **Add Topping:**
     - Brush the dough edges with the beaten egg and sprinkle with coarse sugar.
7. **Bake:**
     - Bake for 35-40 minutes, or until the crust is golden brown and the filling is bubbly.
8. **Cool and Serve:**
     - Allow the galette to cool slightly before slicing and serving.

This fruit galette is delicious on its own or served with a scoop of vanilla ice cream. Enjoy!

Rounds of Focaccia

Ingredients:

For the Dough:

- 4 cups (500g) all-purpose flour
- 1 1/2 cups (360ml) warm water (110°F / 45°C)
- 1/4 cup (60ml) olive oil (plus extra for drizzling)
- 2 tsp salt
- 1 tsp sugar
- 2 tsp active dry yeast

For Topping:

- Fresh rosemary leaves
- Coarse sea salt
- Optional: Cherry tomatoes, olives, or caramelized onions

Instructions:

1. **Prepare the Dough:**
    - In a small bowl, dissolve the sugar in the warm water. Sprinkle the yeast over the top and let it sit for about 5-10 minutes, until frothy.
    - In a large bowl, combine the flour and salt.
    - Make a well in the center and add the yeast mixture and olive oil.
    - Mix until a sticky dough forms. Adjust with more flour or water if necessary.
2. **Knead the Dough:**
    - Turn the dough onto a floured surface and knead for about 8-10 minutes, until smooth and elastic. Alternatively, use a stand mixer with a dough hook for 6-8 minutes.
3. **First Rise:**
    - Place the dough in a lightly oiled bowl, cover with plastic wrap or a damp cloth, and let it rise in a warm place for 1-1.5 hours, or until doubled in size.
4. **Shape the Rounds:**
    - Preheat your oven to 425°F (220°C).
    - Punch down the dough and turn it out onto a floured surface.
    - Divide the dough into 6-8 equal portions and shape each into a round, about 1/2 inch (1.5 cm) thick.
    - Place the rounds on a parchment-lined baking sheet.
5. **Add Toppings:**
    - Dimple each round with your fingers.
    - Drizzle with olive oil, sprinkle with coarse sea salt, and top with fresh rosemary. Add any additional toppings like cherry tomatoes or olives if desired.

6. **Second Rise:**
   - Let the rounds rise for another 20-30 minutes, covered with a cloth.
7. **Bake:**
   - Bake for 15-20 minutes, or until golden brown and the crust is crisp.
8. **Cool and Serve:**
   - Allow the focaccia rounds to cool slightly on a wire rack before serving.

These rounds of focaccia are perfect for serving at parties or as an accompaniment to soups and salads. Enjoy!

Focaccia alla Genovese

Ingredients:

For the Dough:

- 4 cups (500g) all-purpose flour
- 1 1/2 cups (360ml) warm water (110°F / 45°C)
- 1/4 cup (60ml) extra-virgin olive oil (plus extra for drizzling)
- 2 tsp salt
- 1 tsp sugar
- 2 tsp active dry yeast

For Topping:

- 1/4 cup (60ml) extra-virgin olive oil
- Coarse sea salt
- Fresh rosemary leaves (optional)

Instructions:

1. **Prepare the Dough:**
   - In a small bowl, dissolve the sugar in the warm water. Sprinkle the yeast over the top and let it sit for about 5-10 minutes, until frothy.
   - In a large bowl, combine the flour and salt.
   - Make a well in the center and add the yeast mixture and 1/4 cup olive oil.
   - Mix until a sticky dough forms. Adjust with more flour or water if needed.
2. **Knead the Dough:**
   - Turn the dough onto a floured surface and knead for about 8-10 minutes, until smooth and elastic. Alternatively, use a stand mixer with a dough hook for 6-8 minutes.
3. **First Rise:**
   - Place the dough in a lightly oiled bowl, cover with plastic wrap or a damp cloth, and let it rise in a warm place for 1-1.5 hours, or until doubled in size.
4. **Shape the Focaccia:**
   - Preheat your oven to 450°F (230°C).
   - Punch down the dough and transfer it to a parchment-lined baking sheet.
   - Stretch and press the dough out to fit the sheet, about 1/2 inch (1.5 cm) thick.
5. **Add Toppings:**
   - Dimple the surface of the dough with your fingers.
   - Drizzle generously with olive oil, sprinkle with coarse sea salt, and add fresh rosemary if using.
6. **Second Rise:**
   - Let the dough rise for another 20-30 minutes, covered with a cloth.

7. **Bake:**
    - Bake for 20-25 minutes, or until the focaccia is golden brown and the edges are crispy.
8. **Cool and Serve:**
    - Allow the focaccia to cool slightly on a wire rack before slicing.

Focaccia alla Genovese is delicious on its own or paired with a variety of toppings. Enjoy!

Pane con Olio

Ingredients:

For the Dough:

- 4 cups (500g) all-purpose flour
- 1 1/2 cups (360ml) warm water (110°F / 45°C)
- 1/4 cup (60ml) extra-virgin olive oil (plus extra for brushing)
- 2 tsp salt
- 1 tsp sugar
- 2 tsp active dry yeast

For Topping (Optional):

- Coarse sea salt
- Fresh rosemary or thyme leaves

Instructions:

1. **Prepare the Dough:**
    - In a small bowl, dissolve the sugar in the warm water. Sprinkle the yeast over the top and let it sit for about 5-10 minutes, until frothy.
    - In a large bowl, combine the flour and salt.
    - Make a well in the center and add the yeast mixture and 1/4 cup olive oil.
    - Mix until a sticky dough forms. Adjust with more flour or water if needed.
2. **Knead the Dough:**
    - Turn the dough onto a floured surface and knead for about 8-10 minutes, until smooth and elastic. Alternatively, use a stand mixer with a dough hook for 6-8 minutes.
3. **First Rise:**
    - Place the dough in a lightly oiled bowl, cover with plastic wrap or a damp cloth, and let it rise in a warm place for 1-1.5 hours, or until doubled in size.
4. **Shape the Bread:**
    - Preheat your oven to 450°F (230°C).
    - Punch down the dough and transfer it to a floured surface.
    - Shape the dough into a round or oval loaf.
    - Place the shaped dough onto a parchment-lined or floured baking sheet.
5. **Add Toppings:**
    - Optional: Dimple the surface of the dough with your fingers.
    - Brush the top with extra-virgin olive oil and sprinkle with coarse sea salt and fresh herbs if desired.
6. **Second Rise:**
    - Let the dough rise for another 20-30 minutes, covered with a cloth.

7. **Bake:**
   - Bake for 25-30 minutes, or until the bread is golden brown and sounds hollow when tapped on the bottom.
8. **Cool and Serve:**
   - Allow the bread to cool on a wire rack before slicing.

Pane con Olio is perfect for enjoying with a drizzle of high-quality olive oil, and it's great for dipping or as a side to any meal. Enjoy!

Pane Integrale

Ingredients:

- 2 1/2 cups (320g) whole wheat flour
- 1 cup (120g) all-purpose flour
- 1 1/2 cups (360ml) warm water (110°F / 45°C)
- 1/4 cup (60ml) olive oil
- 2 tsp salt
- 2 tbsp honey or molasses
- 2 tsp active dry yeast

Instructions:

1. **Prepare the Yeast Mixture:**
    - In a small bowl, dissolve the honey or molasses in the warm water. Sprinkle the yeast over the top and let it sit for about 5-10 minutes, until frothy.
2. **Prepare the Dough:**
    - In a large bowl, combine the whole wheat flour, all-purpose flour, and salt.
    - Make a well in the center and add the yeast mixture and olive oil.
    - Mix until a sticky dough forms. Adjust with more flour or water if necessary.
3. **Knead the Dough:**
    - Turn the dough onto a floured surface and knead for about 8-10 minutes, until smooth and elastic. Alternatively, use a stand mixer with a dough hook for 6-8 minutes.
4. **First Rise:**
    - Place the dough in a lightly oiled bowl, cover with plastic wrap or a damp cloth, and let it rise in a warm place for 1-1.5 hours, or until doubled in size.
5. **Shape the Bread:**
    - Punch down the dough and turn it out onto a floured surface.
    - Shape the dough into a loaf and place it in a greased 9x5-inch (23x13 cm) loaf pan.
6. **Second Rise:**
    - Cover the loaf with a cloth and let it rise for another 30-45 minutes, or until it has risen above the edge of the pan.
7. **Preheat the Oven:**
    - Preheat your oven to 350°F (175°C).
8. **Bake:**
    - Bake for 30-35 minutes, or until the loaf is golden brown and sounds hollow when tapped on the bottom.
9. **Cool and Serve:**
    - Allow the bread to cool in the pan for about 10 minutes, then transfer to a wire rack to cool completely before slicing.

Pane Integrale is great for sandwiches or enjoyed with a bit of butter or cheese. Enjoy your wholesome bread!

Pizza Margherita Crust

Ingredients:

- 2 1/4 cups (280g) all-purpose flour
- 1 cup (240ml) warm water (110°F / 45°C)
- 2 tbsp olive oil
- 1 tsp salt
- 1 tsp sugar
- 2 tsp active dry yeast

Instructions:

1. **Prepare the Yeast Mixture:**
    - In a small bowl, dissolve the sugar in the warm water. Sprinkle the yeast over the top and let it sit for about 5-10 minutes, or until frothy.
2. **Prepare the Dough:**
    - In a large bowl, combine the flour and salt.
    - Make a well in the center and add the yeast mixture and olive oil.
    - Mix until a dough forms. Adjust with more flour or water if needed.
3. **Knead the Dough:**
    - Turn the dough onto a floured surface and knead for about 8-10 minutes, until smooth and elastic. Alternatively, use a stand mixer with a dough hook for 6-8 minutes.
4. **First Rise:**
    - Place the dough in a lightly oiled bowl, cover with plastic wrap or a damp cloth, and let it rise in a warm place for 1-1.5 hours, or until doubled in size.
5. **Shape the Dough:**
    - Preheat your oven to 475°F (245°C). If using a pizza stone, place it in the oven to preheat.
    - Punch down the dough and turn it out onto a floured surface.
    - Divide the dough into 1 or 2 portions, depending on your desired pizza size.
    - Roll out or stretch each portion into a round shape, about 1/4 inch (0.6 cm) thick.
6. **Pre-Bake (Optional for Crispier Crust):**
    - Transfer the rolled-out dough to a pizza peel or baking sheet.
    - Bake for 5-7 minutes, or until just beginning to set but not browned.
7. **Add Toppings and Bake:**
    - Remove the crust from the oven, add your Margherita toppings (tomato sauce, fresh mozzarella, and basil), and return to the oven.
    - Bake for 10-12 minutes, or until the crust is golden brown and the cheese is bubbly.
8. **Cool and Serve:**
    - Allow the pizza to cool slightly before slicing.

Enjoy your homemade Pizza Margherita with its classic, crispy crust!

Pane di Cirié

Ingredients:

- 3 cups (375g) all-purpose flour
- 1 1/4 cups (300ml) warm water (110°F / 45°C)
- 1/4 cup (60ml) olive oil
- 1 1/2 tsp salt
- 1 tsp sugar
- 2 tsp active dry yeast

Instructions:

1. **Prepare the Yeast Mixture:**
    - In a small bowl, dissolve the sugar in the warm water. Sprinkle the yeast over the top and let it sit for about 5-10 minutes, until frothy.
2. **Prepare the Dough:**
    - In a large bowl, combine the flour and salt.
    - Make a well in the center and add the yeast mixture and olive oil.
    - Mix until a sticky dough forms. Adjust with more flour or water if needed.
3. **Knead the Dough:**
    - Turn the dough onto a floured surface and knead for about 8-10 minutes, until smooth and elastic. Alternatively, use a stand mixer with a dough hook for 6-8 minutes.
4. **First Rise:**
    - Place the dough in a lightly oiled bowl, cover with plastic wrap or a damp cloth, and let it rise in a warm place for 1-1.5 hours, or until doubled in size.
5. **Shape the Bread:**
    - Preheat your oven to 425°F (220°C).
    - Punch down the dough and turn it out onto a floured surface.
    - Shape the dough into a round loaf or divide it into smaller loaves.
6. **Second Rise:**
    - Place the shaped dough onto a parchment-lined or floured baking sheet.
    - Cover with a cloth and let it rise for another 30-45 minutes.
7. **Bake:**
    - Bake for 25-30 minutes, or until the bread is golden brown and sounds hollow when tapped on the bottom.
8. **Cool and Serve:**
    - Allow the bread to cool on a wire rack before slicing.

Pane di Cirié is great for sandwiches, with soups, or simply enjoyed with a bit of olive oil. Buon appetito!

Pan Carré

Ingredients:

- 3 1/2 cups (440g) all-purpose flour
- 1 1/2 cups (360ml) warm water (110°F / 45°C)
- 1/4 cup (60ml) vegetable oil or melted butter
- 2 tbsp sugar
- 2 tsp salt
- 2 tsp active dry yeast

Instructions:

1. **Prepare the Yeast Mixture:**
   - In a small bowl, dissolve the sugar in the warm water. Sprinkle the yeast over the top and let it sit for about 5-10 minutes, or until frothy.
2. **Prepare the Dough:**
   - In a large bowl, combine the flour and salt.
   - Make a well in the center and add the yeast mixture and vegetable oil.
   - Mix until a sticky dough forms. Adjust with more flour or water if needed.
3. **Knead the Dough:**
   - Turn the dough onto a floured surface and knead for about 8-10 minutes, until smooth and elastic. Alternatively, use a stand mixer with a dough hook for 6-8 minutes.
4. **First Rise:**
   - Place the dough in a lightly oiled bowl, cover with plastic wrap or a damp cloth, and let it rise in a warm place for 1-1.5 hours, or until doubled in size.
5. **Shape the Dough:**
   - Preheat your oven to 375°F (190°C).
   - Punch down the dough and turn it out onto a floured surface.
   - Shape the dough into a rectangle that fits into a greased 9x5-inch (23x13 cm) loaf pan, or divide into smaller portions for individual loaves.
6. **Second Rise:**
   - Place the shaped dough into the greased loaf pan.
   - Cover with a cloth and let it rise for another 30-45 minutes, or until it has risen above the edge of the pan.
7. **Bake:**
   - Bake for 30-35 minutes, or until the loaf is golden brown and sounds hollow when tapped on the bottom.
8. **Cool and Serve:**
   - Allow the bread to cool in the pan for about 10 minutes, then transfer to a wire rack to cool completely before slicing.

Pan Carré is excellent for sandwiches, toast, or just enjoyed with a bit of butter. Enjoy your homemade bread!

Focaccia al Pomodoro

Ingredients:

For the Dough:

- 500g (4 cups) all-purpose flour
- 10g (2 teaspoons) salt
- 7g (1 packet) active dry yeast
- 350ml (1 ½ cups) warm water (about 110°F/45°C)
- 3 tablespoons olive oil, plus extra for drizzling

For the Topping:

- 200g (7 oz) cherry tomatoes, halved
- 2 tablespoons olive oil
- 2 cloves garlic, minced
- 1 tablespoon fresh rosemary leaves, chopped (or 1 teaspoon dried rosemary)
- 1 teaspoon dried oregano
- Salt and black pepper to taste
- Optional: a few fresh basil leaves for garnish

Instructions:

1. **Prepare the Dough:**
    - In a small bowl, dissolve the yeast in warm water. Let it sit for about 5 minutes until frothy.
    - In a large bowl, combine the flour and salt.
    - Make a well in the center of the flour and pour in the yeast mixture and olive oil.
    - Mix until the dough starts to come together, then turn it out onto a floured surface and knead for about 8-10 minutes, until smooth and elastic.
    - Place the dough in a lightly oiled bowl, cover with a damp cloth or plastic wrap, and let it rise in a warm place for about 1 hour, or until doubled in size.
2. **Prepare the Topping:**
    - Preheat your oven to 220°C (425°F).
    - In a small bowl, combine the cherry tomatoes, minced garlic, olive oil, rosemary, oregano, salt, and pepper.
3. **Assemble the Focaccia:**
    - Once the dough has risen, punch it down and transfer it to a lightly oiled baking sheet or a 9x13-inch baking pan.
    - Stretch and press the dough out to fit the pan, creating dimples all over the surface with your fingers.
    - Evenly distribute the tomato mixture over the dough, pressing the tomatoes gently into the surface.

4. **Bake:**
    - Bake in the preheated oven for 20-25 minutes, or until the focaccia is golden brown and the tomatoes are roasted.
    - Remove from the oven and let it cool slightly on a wire rack.
5. **Serve:**
    - Garnish with fresh basil leaves if desired.
    - Slice and enjoy warm or at room temperature.

This focaccia is great as an appetizer, a side dish, or even on its own with a drizzle of extra olive oil. Enjoy!

Pane di Orzo

Ingredients:

- 250g (2 cups) barley flour
- 250g (2 cups) all-purpose flour
- 1 packet (7g) active dry yeast
- 300ml (1 ¼ cups) warm water
- 2 tablespoons olive oil
- 1 tablespoon honey
- 1 teaspoon salt

Instructions:

1. **Prepare the Dough:**
   - Dissolve the yeast in warm water and let it sit for about 5 minutes until frothy.
   - In a large bowl, mix the barley flour, all-purpose flour, and salt.
   - Make a well in the center and add the yeast mixture, olive oil, and honey.
   - Stir until the dough begins to come together, then knead on a floured surface for about 8-10 minutes until smooth.
2. **First Rise:**
   - Place the dough in a lightly oiled bowl, cover with a damp cloth, and let it rise in a warm place for about 1 hour, or until doubled in size.
3. **Shape and Second Rise:**
   - Punch down the dough and shape it into a loaf or round shape.
   - Place it on a baking sheet or in a greased loaf pan.
   - Cover and let it rise for another 30 minutes.
4. **Bake:**
   - Preheat your oven to 220°C (425°F).
   - Bake for 25-30 minutes, or until the bread is golden brown and sounds hollow when tapped.
5. **Cool:**
   - Let the bread cool on a wire rack before slicing.

Enjoy the nutty flavor of this wholesome bread!

Pan di Zucchero

Ingredients:

- 500g (4 cups) all-purpose flour
- 200g (1 cup) granulated sugar
- 1 packet (7g) active dry yeast
- 250ml (1 cup) warm milk
- 2 large eggs
- 100g (7 tablespoons) unsalted butter, softened
- 1 teaspoon vanilla extract
- 1/2 teaspoon salt
- Optional: a bit of extra sugar for sprinkling on top

Instructions:

1. **Prepare the Dough:**
   - In a small bowl, dissolve the yeast in warm milk and let it sit for about 5 minutes, or until frothy.
   - In a large bowl, combine the flour, sugar, and salt.
   - Make a well in the center of the dry ingredients and add the yeast mixture, eggs, butter, and vanilla extract.
   - Mix until the dough starts to come together. Turn it out onto a floured surface and knead for about 8-10 minutes until smooth and elastic.
2. **First Rise:**
   - Place the dough in a lightly oiled bowl, cover with a damp cloth or plastic wrap, and let it rise in a warm place for about 1 hour, or until doubled in size.
3. **Shape and Second Rise:**
   - Punch down the dough and shape it into a loaf or divide it into smaller portions for individual rolls.
   - Place the shaped dough on a baking sheet or in a greased loaf pan.
   - Cover and let it rise for another 30 minutes.
4. **Preheat Oven:**
   - Preheat your oven to 180°C (350°F).
5. **Bake:**
   - If desired, sprinkle a little extra sugar on top of the dough before baking.
   - Bake for 25-30 minutes, or until the bread is golden brown and sounds hollow when tapped.
6. **Cool:**
   - Let the bread cool on a wire rack before slicing.

Pan di Zucchero is delightful on its own or with a bit of butter or jam. Enjoy!

Crescia

Ingredients:

- 500g (4 cups) all-purpose flour
- 100g (1 cup) grated Pecorino Romano or Parmesan cheese
- 100g (7 tablespoons) unsalted butter, softened
- 4 large eggs
- 100ml (1/2 cup) milk
- 1 packet (7g) active dry yeast
- 2 tablespoons sugar
- 1 teaspoon salt
- 1 tablespoon olive oil

Instructions:

1. **Prepare the Dough:**
    - In a small bowl, dissolve the yeast in warm milk (about 110°F/45°C) with the sugar. Let it sit for about 5 minutes, or until frothy.
    - In a large bowl, combine the flour, salt, and grated cheese.
    - Make a well in the center and add the yeast mixture, eggs, and softened butter.
    - Mix until the dough begins to come together, then turn it out onto a floured surface and knead for about 10 minutes until smooth and elastic.
2. **First Rise:**
    - Place the dough in a lightly oiled bowl, cover with a damp cloth or plastic wrap, and let it rise in a warm place for about 1 hour, or until doubled in size.
3. **Shape and Second Rise:**
    - Punch down the dough and shape it into a round loaf or divide it into smaller portions if you prefer individual pieces.
    - Place the shaped dough on a baking sheet lined with parchment paper or in a greased round cake pan.
    - Cover and let it rise for another 30-45 minutes.
4. **Preheat Oven:**
    - Preheat your oven to 180°C (350°F).
5. **Bake:**
    - Brush the top of the dough with a little olive oil.
    - Bake for 35-45 minutes, or until the Crescia is golden brown and sounds hollow when tapped.
6. **Cool:**
    - Allow the bread to cool on a wire rack before slicing.

Crescia is great on its own or served with meats, cheeses, or even a simple salad. Enjoy your homemade Crescia!

Focaccia alla Barese

Ingredients:

For the Dough:

- 500g (4 cups) all-purpose flour
- 300ml (1 ¼ cups) warm water
- 10g (2 teaspoons) salt
- 7g (1 packet) active dry yeast
- 3 tablespoons olive oil, plus extra for drizzling

For the Topping:

- 200g (1 cup) cherry tomatoes, halved
- 100g (¾ cup) black olives, pitted and sliced
- 2 tablespoons olive oil
- 1 tablespoon fresh rosemary leaves (or 1 teaspoon dried)
- 1 teaspoon dried oregano
- Salt to taste

Instructions:

1. **Prepare the Dough:**
   - Dissolve the yeast in warm water and let it sit for 5 minutes until frothy.
   - In a large bowl, mix the flour and salt.
   - Make a well in the center, then add the yeast mixture and olive oil.
   - Mix until the dough comes together, then knead on a floured surface for about 8-10 minutes until smooth and elastic.
2. **First Rise:**
   - Place the dough in a lightly oiled bowl, cover with a damp cloth, and let it rise in a warm place for 1 hour or until doubled in size.
3. **Prepare the Topping:**
   - Preheat your oven to 220°C (425°F).
   - In a bowl, combine cherry tomatoes, olives, olive oil, rosemary, oregano, and salt.
4. **Assemble the Focaccia:**
   - Punch down the dough and transfer it to a lightly oiled baking sheet.
   - Stretch and press the dough to fit the sheet, creating dimples with your fingers.
   - Evenly distribute the tomato and olive mixture over the dough, pressing it in slightly.
5. **Second Rise:**
   - Let the dough rise again for about 30 minutes.
6. **Bake:**
   - Bake for 20-25 minutes, or until golden brown and crispy.

7. **Cool:**
    - Allow it to cool slightly before slicing.

Enjoy this savory, flavorful focaccia as an appetizer or a side!

Pane al Vino

Ingredients:

- 500g (4 cups) all-purpose flour
- 200ml (¾ cup) red or white wine
- 100ml (½ cup) warm water
- 7g (1 packet) active dry yeast
- 50g (¼ cup) olive oil
- 2 tablespoons sugar
- 1 teaspoon salt

Instructions:

1. **Prepare the Dough:**
    - Dissolve the yeast and sugar in warm water. Let it sit for about 5 minutes until frothy.
    - In a large bowl, mix the flour and salt.
    - Make a well in the center and add the yeast mixture, wine, and olive oil.
    - Mix until a dough forms, then turn it out onto a floured surface and knead for about 8-10 minutes until smooth.
2. **First Rise:**
    - Place the dough in a lightly oiled bowl, cover with a damp cloth or plastic wrap, and let it rise in a warm place for 1 hour, or until doubled in size.
3. **Shape and Second Rise:**
    - Punch down the dough and shape it into a loaf or round shape.
    - Place it on a baking sheet or in a greased loaf pan.
    - Cover and let it rise for another 30 minutes.
4. **Preheat Oven:**
    - Preheat your oven to 220°C (425°F).
5. **Bake:**
    - Bake for 25-30 minutes, or until the bread is golden brown and sounds hollow when tapped.
6. **Cool:**
    - Let the bread cool on a wire rack before slicing.

This wine-infused bread pairs wonderfully with cheeses, charcuterie, or simply enjoyed on its own. Enjoy!

Pan di Spagna

Ingredients:

- 4 large eggs
- 120g (½ cup) granulated sugar
- 120g (1 cup) all-purpose flour
- 1 teaspoon vanilla extract
- 1/2 teaspoon baking powder (optional, for extra fluffiness)
- A pinch of salt

Instructions:

1. **Preheat Oven:**
    - Preheat your oven to 180°C (350°F). Grease and flour an 8-inch round cake pan or line it with parchment paper.
2. **Prepare the Batter:**
    - In a large bowl, beat the eggs with sugar using an electric mixer on high speed for about 5 minutes, or until thick and pale.
    - Gently fold in the flour, salt, and baking powder (if using) in small batches. Add vanilla extract.
    - Be careful not to deflate the batter; use a light hand.
3. **Bake:**
    - Pour the batter into the prepared pan and smooth the top.
    - Bake for 25-30 minutes, or until the cake is golden and a toothpick inserted into the center comes out clean.
4. **Cool:**
    - Let the cake cool in the pan for 10 minutes, then transfer to a wire rack to cool completely.

This sponge cake is ideal for making layered cakes or serving with fruit and cream. Enjoy!

Pane di Patate

Ingredients:

- 500g (4 cups) all-purpose flour
- 200g (1 cup) mashed potatoes (about 2 medium potatoes)
- 200ml (¾ cup) warm water
- 7g (1 packet) active dry yeast
- 50g (¼ cup) unsalted butter, softened
- 2 tablespoons olive oil
- 1 tablespoon sugar
- 1 teaspoon salt

Instructions:

1. **Prepare the Dough:**
   - In a small bowl, dissolve the yeast and sugar in warm water. Let it sit for about 5 minutes until frothy.
   - In a large bowl, combine the flour and salt.
   - Make a well in the center of the dry ingredients and add the yeast mixture, mashed potatoes, butter, and olive oil.
   - Mix until the dough comes together, then turn it out onto a floured surface and knead for about 8-10 minutes until smooth and elastic.
2. **First Rise:**
   - Place the dough in a lightly oiled bowl, cover with a damp cloth or plastic wrap, and let it rise in a warm place for about 1 hour, or until doubled in size.
3. **Shape and Second Rise:**
   - Punch down the dough and shape it into a loaf or divide it into smaller portions for rolls.
   - Place the shaped dough on a baking sheet or in a greased loaf pan.
   - Cover and let it rise for another 30-45 minutes.
4. **Preheat Oven:**
   - Preheat your oven to 220°C (425°F).
5. **Bake:**
   - Bake for 25-30 minutes, or until the bread is golden brown and sounds hollow when tapped.
6. **Cool:**
   - Allow the bread to cool on a wire rack before slicing.

This Pane di Patate is wonderfully moist and pairs well with a variety of dishes or can be enjoyed on its own. Enjoy your homemade potato bread!

Focaccia con Cipolle

Ingredients:

For the Dough:

- 500g (4 cups) all-purpose flour
- 300ml (1 ¼ cups) warm water
- 7g (1 packet) active dry yeast
- 10g (2 teaspoons) salt
- 3 tablespoons olive oil, plus extra for drizzling

For the Topping:

- 2 large onions, thinly sliced
- 2 tablespoons olive oil
- 1 tablespoon fresh rosemary leaves (or 1 teaspoon dried)
- 1 teaspoon sugar
- Salt and black pepper to taste

Instructions:

1. **Prepare the Dough:**
   - Dissolve the yeast in warm water and let it sit for 5 minutes until frothy.
   - In a large bowl, mix the flour and salt.
   - Make a well in the center and add the yeast mixture and olive oil.
   - Mix until the dough begins to come together, then knead on a floured surface for about 8-10 minutes until smooth.
2. **First Rise:**
   - Place the dough in a lightly oiled bowl, cover with a damp cloth, and let it rise in a warm place for about 1 hour, or until doubled in size.
3. **Prepare the Topping:**
   - Heat olive oil in a pan over medium heat. Add the onions and sugar, and cook, stirring occasionally, until the onions are caramelized, about 15-20 minutes. Season with salt and pepper.
4. **Assemble the Focaccia:**
   - Preheat your oven to 220°C (425°F).
   - Punch down the dough and transfer it to a lightly oiled baking sheet. Stretch and press the dough to fit the sheet, creating dimples with your fingers.
   - Spread the caramelized onions evenly over the dough and sprinkle with rosemary.
5. **Second Rise:**
   - Let the dough rise for another 30 minutes.
6. **Bake:**

- ○ Drizzle a bit of olive oil over the top.
- ○ Bake for 20-25 minutes, or until golden brown.
7. **Cool:**
   - ○ Let it cool slightly before slicing.

This focaccia is perfect as an appetizer, side dish, or even a light meal on its own. Enjoy!

Focaccia al Rosmarino e Sale Grosso

Ingredients:

For the Dough:

- 500g (4 cups) all-purpose flour
- 300ml (1 ¼ cups) warm water
- 7g (1 packet) active dry yeast
- 10g (2 teaspoons) salt
- 3 tablespoons olive oil, plus extra for drizzling

For the Topping:

- 2 tablespoons fresh rosemary leaves (or 1 tablespoon dried)
- 2-3 tablespoons coarse sea salt
- 2-3 tablespoons olive oil

Instructions:

1. **Prepare the Dough:**
    - Dissolve the yeast in warm water and let it sit for 5 minutes until frothy.
    - In a large bowl, mix the flour and salt.
    - Make a well in the center and add the yeast mixture and olive oil.
    - Mix until the dough comes together, then knead on a floured surface for about 8-10 minutes until smooth.
2. **First Rise:**
    - Place the dough in a lightly oiled bowl, cover with a damp cloth or plastic wrap, and let it rise in a warm place for about 1 hour, or until doubled in size.
3. **Assemble the Focaccia:**
    - Preheat your oven to 220°C (425°F).
    - Punch down the dough and transfer it to a lightly oiled baking sheet.
    - Stretch and press the dough to fit the sheet, creating dimples with your fingers.
    - Drizzle olive oil over the top, then sprinkle with rosemary and coarse sea salt.
4. **Second Rise:**
    - Let the dough rise for another 30 minutes.
5. **Bake:**
    - Bake for 20-25 minutes, or until golden brown.
6. **Cool:**
    - Allow to cool slightly before slicing.

This focaccia is perfect as a side dish or enjoyed on its own. Buon appetito!

Pane di Biga

Ingredients:

For the Biga:

- 150g (1 cup) all-purpose flour
- 100ml (⅓ cup + 1 tablespoon) water
- 1/4 teaspoon active dry yeast

For the Dough:

- 350g (2 ¾ cups) all-purpose flour
- 200ml (¾ cup + 2 tablespoons) water
- 10g (2 teaspoons) salt
- 1 packet (7g) active dry yeast
- 1 tablespoon olive oil

Instructions:

1. **Prepare the Biga:**
    - In a small bowl, mix the flour, water, and yeast until well combined.
    - Cover and let it sit at room temperature for 12-16 hours, or until bubbly and expanded.
2. **Prepare the Dough:**
    - In a large bowl, combine the flour and salt.
    - Dissolve the yeast in warm water and let it sit for 5 minutes.
    - Add the yeast mixture, olive oil, and the prepared biga to the flour.
    - Mix until the dough forms, then turn it out onto a floured surface and knead for about 8-10 minutes until smooth.
3. **First Rise:**
    - Place the dough in a lightly oiled bowl, cover with a damp cloth or plastic wrap, and let it rise in a warm place for about 1 hour, or until doubled in size.
4. **Shape and Second Rise:**
    - Punch down the dough and shape it into a loaf or round shape.
    - Place it on a baking sheet or in a greased loaf pan.
    - Cover and let it rise for another 30-45 minutes.
5. **Preheat Oven:**
    - Preheat your oven to 220°C (425°F).
6. **Bake:**
    - Bake for 25-30 minutes, or until the bread is golden brown and sounds hollow when tapped.
7. **Cool:**
    - Let the bread cool on a wire rack before slicing.

This bread has a lovely texture and flavor thanks to the biga. Enjoy it fresh or with your favorite spreads!

Focaccia con Olive

Ingredients:

For the Dough:

- 500g (4 cups) all-purpose flour
- 300ml (1 ¼ cups) warm water
- 7g (1 packet) active dry yeast
- 10g (2 teaspoons) salt
- 3 tablespoons olive oil, plus extra for drizzling

For the Topping:

- 100g (¾ cup) black or green olives, pitted and sliced
- 2 tablespoons olive oil
- 1 tablespoon fresh rosemary leaves (or 1 teaspoon dried)
- 1 teaspoon coarse sea salt

Instructions:

1. **Prepare the Dough:**
    - Dissolve the yeast in warm water and let it sit for about 5 minutes until frothy.
    - In a large bowl, mix the flour and salt.
    - Make a well in the center and add the yeast mixture and olive oil.
    - Mix until the dough comes together, then knead on a floured surface for about 8-10 minutes until smooth and elastic.
2. **First Rise:**
    - Place the dough in a lightly oiled bowl, cover with a damp cloth or plastic wrap, and let it rise in a warm place for about 1 hour, or until doubled in size.
3. **Assemble the Focaccia:**
    - Preheat your oven to 220°C (425°F).
    - Punch down the dough and transfer it to a lightly oiled baking sheet.
    - Stretch and press the dough to fit the sheet, creating dimples with your fingers.
    - Drizzle olive oil over the top, then scatter the sliced olives evenly.
    - Sprinkle with rosemary and coarse sea salt.
4. **Second Rise:**
    - Let the dough rise for another 30 minutes.
5. **Bake:**
    - Bake for 20-25 minutes, or until golden brown and crispy.
6. **Cool:**
    - Allow to cool slightly before slicing.

This focaccia pairs wonderfully with cheese, cured meats, or can be enjoyed on its own. Buon appetito!

Pane alla Pugliese

Ingredients:

For the Biga (Preferment):

- 150g (1 cup) all-purpose flour
- 100ml (⅓ cup + 1 tablespoon) water
- 1/4 teaspoon active dry yeast

For the Dough:

- 350g (2 ¾ cups) all-purpose flour
- 200ml (¾ cup + 2 tablespoons) water
- 1 packet (7g) active dry yeast
- 10g (2 teaspoons) salt
- 2 tablespoons olive oil
- Optional: 1 tablespoon honey or sugar (for a slight sweetness)

Instructions:

1. **Prepare the Biga:**
   - In a small bowl, mix the flour, water, and yeast until well combined.
   - Cover and let it sit at room temperature for 12-16 hours, or until bubbly and expanded.
2. **Prepare the Dough:**
   - In a large bowl, combine the flour and salt.
   - Dissolve the yeast in warm water and let it sit for 5 minutes.
   - Add the yeast mixture, olive oil, and the prepared biga to the flour.
   - Mix until the dough forms, then turn it out onto a floured surface and knead for about 10 minutes until smooth and elastic.
3. **First Rise:**
   - Place the dough in a lightly oiled bowl, cover with a damp cloth or plastic wrap, and let it rise in a warm place for about 1 hour, or until doubled in size.
4. **Shape and Second Rise:**
   - Punch down the dough and shape it into a round loaf or divide it into smaller portions for individual loaves.
   - Place it on a baking sheet or in a greased round cake pan.
   - Cover and let it rise for another 30-45 minutes.
5. **Preheat Oven:**
   - Preheat your oven to 220°C (425°F).
6. **Bake:**
   - Optionally, you can make a few shallow cuts on the surface of the dough for a traditional look.

- Bake for 30-35 minutes, or until the bread is golden brown and sounds hollow when tapped.

7. **Cool:**
    - Let the bread cool on a wire rack before slicing.

Pane alla Pugliese is great for sandwiches, alongside soups, or just enjoyed with a drizzle of olive oil. Enjoy your homemade bread!

Pane al Lievito Madre

Ingredients:

For the Lievito Madre (Mother Yeast):

- 100g (¾ cup) all-purpose flour
- 50g (¼ cup) water
- 1/8 teaspoon active dry yeast (optional, to help start the fermentation process)

For the Dough:

- 500g (4 cups) all-purpose flour
- 200ml (¾ cup + 2 tablespoons) water
- 100g (½ cup) Lievito Madre, refreshed and active
- 10g (2 teaspoons) salt
- 30g (2 tablespoons) olive oil

Instructions:

1. **Prepare the Lievito Madre:**
    - In a bowl, mix the flour, water, and yeast (if using).
    - Cover and let it sit at room temperature for 24 hours.
    - After 24 hours, discard half of the mixture and feed it with 100g flour and 50g water. Let it sit for another 24 hours. Repeat this feeding process every day for about 5-7 days until the mixture is bubbly and has a pleasant, slightly sour smell.
2. **Prepare the Dough:**
    - In a large bowl, combine the flour and salt.
    - In another bowl, mix the active Lievito Madre with the water until dissolved.
    - Add the Lievito Madre mixture and olive oil to the flour.
    - Mix until the dough starts to come together, then turn it out onto a floured surface and knead for about 10 minutes until smooth and elastic.
3. **First Rise:**
    - Place the dough in a lightly oiled bowl, cover with a damp cloth or plastic wrap, and let it rise in a warm place for about 1.5 to 2 hours, or until doubled in size.
4. **Shape and Second Rise:**
    - Punch down the dough and shape it into a loaf or round shape.
    - Place the shaped dough on a baking sheet or in a greased loaf pan.
    - Cover and let it rise for another 45 minutes to 1 hour.
5. **Preheat Oven:**
    - Preheat your oven to 220°C (425°F).
6. **Bake:**
    - Optionally, you can make a few shallow cuts on the surface of the dough for a traditional look.
    - Bake for 30-35 minutes, or until the bread is golden brown and sounds hollow when tapped.
7. **Cool:**

- Let the bread cool on a wire rack before slicing.

This bread will have a complex flavor and a lovely texture thanks to the natural leavening. Enjoy it with a variety of dishes or simply with a bit of butter or olive oil!

Focaccia con Aglio

Ingredients:

For the Dough:

- 500g (4 cups) all-purpose flour
- 300ml (1 ¼ cups) warm water
- 7g (1 packet) active dry yeast
- 10g (2 teaspoons) salt
- 3 tablespoons olive oil, plus extra for drizzling

For the Garlic Topping:

- 3-4 cloves garlic, thinly sliced
- 2 tablespoons olive oil
- 1 tablespoon fresh rosemary leaves (or 1 teaspoon dried)
- 1 teaspoon coarse sea salt

Instructions:

1. **Prepare the Dough:**
   - Dissolve the yeast in warm water and let it sit for about 5 minutes until frothy.
   - In a large bowl, mix the flour and salt.
   - Make a well in the center and add the yeast mixture and olive oil.
   - Mix until the dough comes together, then turn it out onto a floured surface and knead for about 8-10 minutes until smooth and elastic.
2. **First Rise:**
   - Place the dough in a lightly oiled bowl, cover with a damp cloth or plastic wrap, and let it rise in a warm place for about 1 hour, or until doubled in size.
3. **Prepare the Garlic Topping:**
   - Heat the olive oil in a small pan over medium heat.
   - Add the garlic slices and cook gently until they are golden and fragrant, about 2-3 minutes. Be careful not to burn them. Remove from heat and set aside.
4. **Assemble the Focaccia:**
   - Preheat your oven to 220°C (425°F).
   - Punch down the dough and transfer it to a lightly oiled baking sheet.
   - Stretch and press the dough to fit the sheet, creating dimples with your fingers.
   - Drizzle a bit of olive oil over the top, then scatter the garlic slices evenly.
   - Sprinkle with rosemary and coarse sea salt.
5. **Second Rise:**
   - Let the dough rise for another 30 minutes.
6. **Bake:**
   - Bake for 20-25 minutes, or until golden brown and crispy.

7. **Cool:**
    - Allow to cool slightly before slicing.

This focaccia is perfect as an appetizer, side dish, or for dipping in olive oil. Enjoy!

Pane alla Griglia

Ingredients:

- 1 loaf of Italian bread (ciabatta, baguette, or a rustic country bread work well)
- 2-3 tablespoons olive oil
- 2-3 cloves garlic, peeled (optional, for rubbing)
- Salt and black pepper, to taste
- Optional toppings: fresh herbs (like rosemary or thyme), grated Parmesan cheese, or a drizzle of balsamic vinegar

Instructions:

1. **Prepare the Bread:**
    - Slice the loaf into 1/2-inch to 1-inch thick slices. You can cut it into rounds, rectangles, or whatever shape you prefer.
2. **Preheat the Grill or Grill Pan:**
    - Preheat your grill to medium-high heat. If using a grill pan, heat it over medium-high heat on the stovetop.
3. **Grill the Bread:**
    - Brush both sides of the bread slices with olive oil.
    - Place the bread slices on the grill or grill pan.
    - Grill for about 2-4 minutes per side, or until the bread is crispy and has nice grill marks. Keep an eye on it to avoid burning.
4. **Add Flavor:**
    - If desired, rub the hot grilled bread with the cut sides of a garlic clove for a subtle garlic flavor.
    - Season with salt and black pepper to taste.
5. **Optional Toppings:**
    - You can add toppings like fresh herbs, grated Parmesan cheese, or a drizzle of balsamic vinegar for extra flavor. If adding cheese, sprinkle it on just before the bread finishes grilling so it can slightly melt.
6. **Serve:**
    - Serve the grilled bread warm, as a side dish, appetizer, or with your favorite dips.

Variations:

- **Bruschetta:** Top with a mixture of diced tomatoes, basil, garlic, olive oil, and salt for a classic bruschetta.
- **Antipasto:** Serve with an assortment of olives, cheeses, and cured meats.

Pane alla Griglia is versatile and easy to prepare, making it a great addition to many meals. Enjoy!

Pan di Mais

Ingredients:

- 250g (2 cups) cornmeal
- 200g (1 ½ cups) all-purpose flour
- 2 teaspoons baking powder
- ½ teaspoon baking soda
- 1 teaspoon salt
- 100g (½ cup) granulated sugar
- 2 large eggs
- 250ml (1 cup) buttermilk or milk
- 100g (¼ cup) unsalted butter, melted
- Optional: 100g (1 cup) corn kernels (fresh, frozen, or canned)

Instructions:

1. **Preheat Oven:**
    - Preheat your oven to 200°C (400°F). Grease or line an 8-inch square baking pan or a similar-sized oven-safe dish.
2. **Prepare Dry Ingredients:**
    - In a large bowl, whisk together the cornmeal, flour, baking powder, baking soda, salt, and sugar.
3. **Prepare Wet Ingredients:**
    - In another bowl, beat the eggs and then mix in the buttermilk and melted butter.
4. **Combine:**
    - Pour the wet ingredients into the dry ingredients and stir until just combined. If using, fold in the corn kernels.
5. **Bake:**
    - Pour the batter into the prepared pan and spread evenly.
    - Bake for 25-30 minutes, or until the top is golden brown and a toothpick inserted into the center comes out clean.
6. **Cool:**
    - Allow the cornbread to cool in the pan for about 10 minutes before slicing.

This Pan di Mais is excellent served warm with a pat of butter or alongside soups and stews. Enjoy!

Focaccia ai Formaggi

Ingredients:

For the Dough:

- 500g (4 cups) all-purpose flour
- 300ml (1 ¼ cups) warm water
- 7g (1 packet) active dry yeast
- 10g (2 teaspoons) salt
- 3 tablespoons olive oil, plus extra for drizzling

For the Cheese Topping:

- 150g (1 ½ cups) shredded mozzarella cheese
- 100g (1 cup) grated Parmesan cheese
- Optional: 100g (1 cup) crumbled goat cheese or feta cheese
- 2 tablespoons fresh rosemary leaves (or 1 teaspoon dried)
- 1 teaspoon coarse sea salt

Instructions:

1. **Prepare the Dough:**
    - Dissolve the yeast in warm water and let it sit for about 5 minutes until frothy.
    - In a large bowl, mix the flour and salt.
    - Make a well in the center and add the yeast mixture and olive oil.
    - Mix until the dough comes together, then turn it out onto a floured surface and knead for about 8-10 minutes until smooth and elastic.
2. **First Rise:**
    - Place the dough in a lightly oiled bowl, cover with a damp cloth or plastic wrap, and let it rise in a warm place for about 1 hour, or until doubled in size.
3. **Assemble the Focaccia:**
    - Preheat your oven to 220°C (425°F).
    - Punch down the dough and transfer it to a lightly oiled baking sheet.
    - Stretch and press the dough to fit the sheet, creating dimples with your fingers.
    - Drizzle a bit of olive oil over the top.
    - Scatter the shredded mozzarella, grated Parmesan, and crumbled goat cheese (if using) evenly over the dough.
    - Sprinkle with rosemary and coarse sea salt.
4. **Second Rise:**
    - Let the dough rise for another 30 minutes.
5. **Bake:**
    - Bake for 20-25 minutes, or until the focaccia is golden brown and the cheese is bubbly and slightly browned.

6. **Cool:**
   - Allow to cool slightly before slicing.

This focaccia is wonderfully cheesy and has a rich flavor from the combination of cheeses. It's perfect for serving as an appetizer, side dish, or snack. Enjoy!

Pane della Nonna

Ingredients:

- 500g (4 cups) all-purpose flour
- 300ml (1 ¼ cups) warm water
- 7g (1 packet) active dry yeast
- 10g (2 teaspoons) salt
- 2 tablespoons olive oil (optional, for added richness)
- 1 tablespoon honey or sugar (optional, to help activate the yeast)

Instructions:

1. **Prepare the Dough:**
   - **Activate the Yeast:** In a small bowl, dissolve the yeast (and honey or sugar, if using) in warm water. Let it sit for about 5 minutes until it becomes frothy.
   - **Mix the Ingredients:** In a large bowl, combine the flour and salt. Make a well in the center.
   - **Combine:** Pour the yeast mixture and olive oil (if using) into the well of the flour. Mix until the dough starts to come together.
   - **Knead:** Turn the dough out onto a floured surface and knead for about 8-10 minutes, until smooth and elastic.
2. **First Rise:**
   - Place the dough in a lightly oiled bowl, cover with a damp cloth or plastic wrap, and let it rise in a warm place for about 1-1.5 hours, or until doubled in size.
3. **Shape and Second Rise:**
   - Punch down the dough and shape it into a round loaf or place it in a greased loaf pan.
   - Cover and let it rise for another 30-45 minutes, or until it has risen again and looks puffy.
4. **Preheat Oven:**
   - Preheat your oven to 220°C (425°F).
5. **Bake:**
   - Optionally, you can make a few shallow cuts on the surface of the dough for a traditional look.
   - Bake for 25-30 minutes, or until the bread is golden brown and sounds hollow when tapped on the bottom.
6. **Cool:**
   - Allow the bread to cool on a wire rack before slicing.

Variations and Tips:

- **Herbs and Cheese:** For added flavor, you can mix in some dried herbs (like rosemary or thyme) or shredded cheese into the dough before the first rise.
- **Crusty Loaf:** To get a crispier crust, place a small oven-safe dish of water in the oven while baking to create steam.

Pane della Nonna is perfect for enjoying with soups, stews, or just a bit of butter. It's a wonderful bread that embodies the simplicity and comfort of traditional Italian home baking. Buon appetito!

Pane alla Romana

Ingredients:

- 500g (4 cups) all-purpose flour
- 300ml (1 ¼ cups) warm water
- 7g (1 packet) active dry yeast
- 10g (2 teaspoons) salt
- 2 tablespoons olive oil (optional, for added richness)

Instructions:

1. **Prepare the Dough:**
   - **Activate the Yeast:** In a small bowl, dissolve the yeast in warm water. Let it sit for about 5 minutes until it becomes frothy.
   - **Mix the Ingredients:** In a large bowl, combine the flour and salt. Make a well in the center.
   - **Combine:** Pour the yeast mixture and olive oil (if using) into the well of the flour. Mix until the dough starts to come together.
   - **Knead:** Turn the dough out onto a floured surface and knead for about 8-10 minutes, until smooth and elastic.
2. **First Rise:**
   - Place the dough in a lightly oiled bowl, cover with a damp cloth or plastic wrap, and let it rise in a warm place for about 1-1.5 hours, or until doubled in size.
3. **Shape and Second Rise:**
   - Punch down the dough and shape it into a round loaf. Place it on a baking sheet lined with parchment paper or in a greased round cake pan.
   - Cover and let it rise for another 30-45 minutes, or until it has risen and looks puffy.
4. **Preheat Oven:**
   - Preheat your oven to 220°C (425°F).
5. **Bake:**
   - Optionally, you can make a few shallow cuts on the surface of the dough for a traditional look.
   - Bake for 25-30 minutes, or until the bread is golden brown and sounds hollow when tapped on the bottom.
6. **Cool:**
   - Allow the bread to cool on a wire rack before slicing.

Tips for the Best Pane alla Romana:

- **Flour:** Use high-quality flour for the best texture. Italian "00" flour or bread flour can give the best results.

- **Steam:** To get a crisper crust, you can place a small oven-safe dish of water in the oven while baking to create steam.

Pane alla Romana is a versatile bread that pairs well with everything from cheeses and cured meats to soups and salads. Enjoy the taste of Rome with this delicious and rustic loaf!

Focaccia alle Erbe

Ingredients:

For the Dough:

- 500g (4 cups) all-purpose flour
- 300ml (1 ¼ cups) warm water
- 7g (1 packet) active dry yeast
- 10g (2 teaspoons) salt
- 3 tablespoons olive oil, plus extra for drizzling

For the Herb Topping:

- 2 tablespoons mixed fresh herbs (such as rosemary, thyme, sage, and oregano), finely chopped
- 3-4 tablespoons olive oil
- 1 teaspoon coarse sea salt

Instructions:

1. **Prepare the Dough:**
    - Dissolve the yeast in warm water and let it sit for about 5 minutes until frothy.
    - In a large bowl, mix the flour and salt.
    - Make a well in the center and add the yeast mixture and olive oil.
    - Mix until the dough comes together, then turn it out onto a floured surface and knead for about 8-10 minutes until smooth and elastic.
2. **First Rise:**
    - Place the dough in a lightly oiled bowl, cover with a damp cloth or plastic wrap, and let it rise in a warm place for about 1 hour, or until doubled in size.
3. **Assemble the Focaccia:**
    - Preheat your oven to 220°C (425°F).
    - Punch down the dough and transfer it to a lightly oiled baking sheet.
    - Stretch and press the dough to fit the sheet, creating dimples with your fingers.
    - Drizzle with olive oil.
    - Sprinkle the chopped herbs evenly over the top and then sprinkle with coarse sea salt.
4. **Second Rise:**
    - Let the dough rise for another 30 minutes.
5. **Bake:**
    - Bake for 20-25 minutes, or until the focaccia is golden brown and crispy on the edges.
6. **Cool:**
    - Allow to cool slightly before slicing.

Focaccia alle Erbe is wonderfully aromatic and versatile, perfect for dipping in olive oil or pairing with cheeses and charcuterie. Enjoy!

www.ingramcontent.com/pod-product-compliance
Lightning Source LLC
LaVergne TN
LVHW061944070526
838199LV00060B/3957